DATE DUE

MAY 1 6 2000		

DATE DUE

NOV 27 1985	AUG 17 1987	JAN 2 5 1994
MAR 2 4 1986	SEP 10 1987	MAY 3 1 1994
APR 22 1986	DEC 4 - 1987	SEP 1 9 1995
OCT 15 1986	MAR 2 1 1988	OCT 17 1995
FEB 1 0 1987	APR 5	FEB 2 0 1996
MAR 30 1987	MAR 2 1 1990	JAN 2 4 1998
APR 13 1987	APR 7 3 1990	MAY 2 8 1998
MAY 16 1987	APR 1 4 1990	
JUN 3 1987	NOV 0 1 1991	MAR 1 0 1998
JUL 1 1987	OCT 2 8 1992	DEC 2 3 1999

A THINGS TO MAKE AND DO BOOK
FRANKLIN WATTS
NEW YORK / LONDON / 1978

Things to Make and Do

for Your Birthday

By Gail Gibbons

To my loving husband, Kent

Library of Congress Cataloging in Publication Data

Gibbons, Gail.
   Things to make and do for your birthday.

   (A Things to make and do book)
   SUMMARY: Includes projects, games, jokes, and
party foods for use in celebrating birthdays.
   1. Handicraft — Juvenile literature. 2. Cookery —
Juvenile literature. 3. Games — Juvenile literature.
4. Birthdays — Juvenile literature. [1. Birthdays.
2. Handicraft. 3. Games. 4. Cookery] I. Title.
TT160.G425   745.59′41   77-15109
ISBN 0-531-01462-2 lib. bdg.
ISBN 0-531-02380-x

Copyright ©1978 by Franklin Watts, Inc.

It's fun to have a birthday party.
But, first, make some gifts for the
friends who will come to your party.
You can ask a friend to help you.
Birthday hats are fun to make.

You need:

Construction paper

Scissors

Tape

A crayon

Make one hat for each friend.

How to do it:

1. Cut one strip of paper that will fit around your head. Tape it. This is the rim of the hat.

2. Cut 10 strips of paper as long as from your elbow to your wrist.

3. Tape each strip from one side of the rim to the other side until the rim is covered.

7

4. Cut another strip to fit around your head. Write "Happy Birthday" and your name on it.

5. Tape it to the outside of the rim.

6. Bend up the edges.

7. Decorate the top of the hat.

Won't your friends be surprised?

In Mexico, children have a piñata at their party. A piñata is a decoration made out of wet, pulpy paper. When it dries, gifts and sweets are put inside. At the party it is hung from the ceiling. The children try to break it with a stick. When it is finally broken, the toys fall out.

You can have a piñata at your birthday party. But you need to make it a few days before the party so it will be ready on time.

You need:

Newspaper

A big balloon

3 cups of whole wheat flour

3¾ cups of water

A mixing bowl

A spoon

Old paper bags

Scissors

How to make it:

1. Spread out the newspaper on the table.

2. Blow up the big balloon.

3. Mix the flour and water in the mixing bowl.

4. Cut the paper bags into about 70 strips. Each strip should fit halfway around the balloon.

5. Take one strip at a time, and dip it into the flour and water. Press it onto the balloon.

6. Keep putting on the strips. Overlap the strips until the balloon is covered EXCEPT FOR ONE END.

7. Save some of the paper bag strips for later.

8. Let the balloon dry for one day and one night.

While the piñata is drying, you can make the gifts to go inside it.

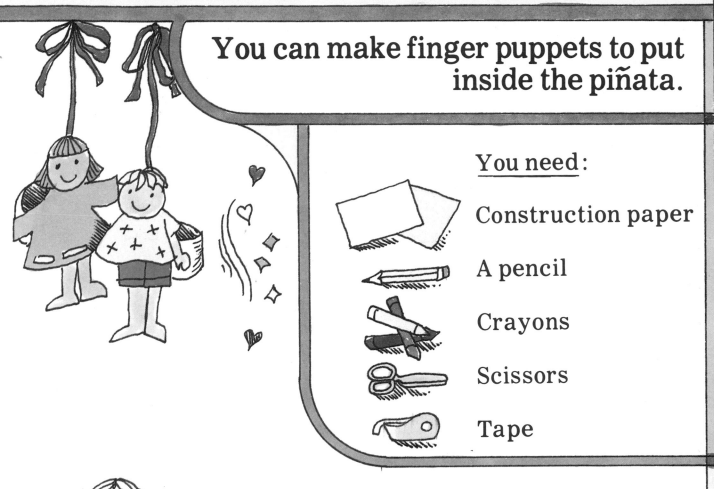

You can make finger puppets to put inside the piñata.

You need:

Construction paper

A pencil

Crayons

Scissors

Tape

1. Draw people about as long as your middle finger. Draw their faces. Make them look like each of the friends you have invited.

2. Draw tabs on them, like this. Crayon them.

3. Cut each figure out.

4. Tape each tab so it fits around your finger.

Now you have finger puppets.

In China, children make fortune cookies. A fortune tells you your future. Each cookie has a small piece of paper baked inside it with a fortune written on it. You can make fortune balloons for your piñata.

You need:

 As many balloons as the number of friends you have invited

 A pencil

 One small piece of paper for each balloon

How to do it:

1. Write a fortune on each piece of paper. Here is an example:

> You will be a space explorer.

2. Put one fortune in each balloon. Don't blow them up.

Now that the piñata is dry, it's time to put the gifts inside. Here's how to do it.

You need:

1 cup of whole wheat flour

1¼ cups of water

A mixing bowl

A spoon

The paper bag strips you have saved

Scissors

How to do it:

1. Mix the flour with the water.

2. Hold the piñata like this.
   Pop the balloon and pull it out.
   Put in the toys and other things.

3. Dip the strips into the flour and water, and seal up the end.

4. Let it dry for one day and one night.

I'm putting in confetti and streamers.

I'm putting in sweets, too.

Now that the piñata is dry again, you can decorate it.

You need:

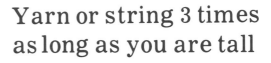 Poster paints

 A big paint brush

 Yarn or string 3 times as long as you are tall

 Thumb tacks

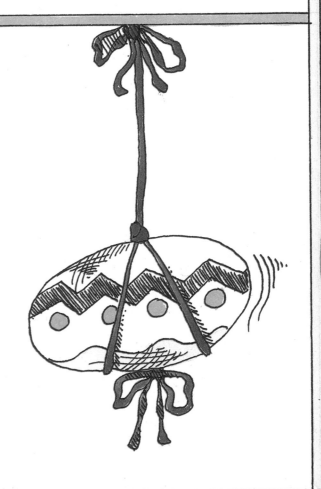

How to do it:

1. Paint the piñata.

2. Make a bow of yarn. Tack it to the bottom of the piñata.

3. Tie some yarn around the top, like this.

18

How many birthday cakes are hidden in this picture?

The answer is on page 48.

When your friends come to the party, give them their hats. Then tell them about the piñata. Have a grownup hold it above your heads. Take turns hitting it with a stick.

The "Birthday Noodles Game" is fun to play with your friends.

<u>You need</u>:

A box of alphabet noodles

<u>How to play</u>:

1. Pour out the box of alphabet noodles onto the table.

2. When you say "Go," each player tries to spell out "Happy Birthday" and your name.

3. The first player done, wins.

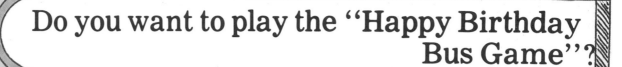

Do you want to play the "Happy Birthday Bus Game"?

You need:

Half as many chairs as players

A table

Each player's name written on a separate piece of paper

How to play:

1. Put the chairs in rows, like a bus.

2. Put the papers with the players' names on them on a table away from the chairs.

3. Since you're the birthday child, you're the bus driver. You say:

   "My Birthday Bus is here,

   Hurry, so we'll be on time.

   Quick, pick up your tickets over there,

   We'll leave when the clock strikes nine."

4. After you have said the poem, your friends run to the table to find their own tickets and quickly run back to you. If they have the right ticket with their own name on it, they can sit on the bus. If not, they have to go back to the table.

5. When the bus is full, the players on the bus say "Gong" nine times and pretend to drive away.

6. The others wave good-bye.

You can play the "Find the Numbers Game."

You need:

A newspaper (an ad section is best)

A pencil for each player

How to play:

1. Give each player a page from the newspaper and a pencil.

2. When you say "Go," each player circles all the numbers that are the same as your birthday age.

3. When the time is up, the player with the most circles wins.

27

Would you like to play the "Balloon Float Contest"?

You need:

Save as many cardboard tubes as friends invited to the party. Paper towel or toilet paper tubes are good.

Blow up as many balloons as friends invited to the party.

How to play:

1. Each player holds a tube up in the air and places a balloon on top of it.

2. When you say "Go," each player tries to keep the balloon floating as long as possible by blowing through the tube.

3. The player who can keep his or her balloon up in the air the longest wins.

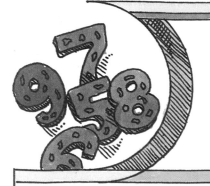

After having the Balloon Float Contest, it would be fun to serve Birthday Numbers Cookies. Make the cookies the day before the party.

You need:

A cardboard stencil of your birthday number

3¼ cups of flour

A saucepan

½ teaspoon baking soda

1 cup of molasses or treacle

1 tablespoon powdered ginger

A mixing bowl

1½ teaspoons salt

A rolling pin

A spoon

A blunt knife

½ cup of butter

A baking sheet

A sifter or sieve

Raisins

How to make 40 cookies:

1. Ask a grownup to set the oven at 350°F.

2. Ask a grownup to boil the molasses (or treacle).

3. Pour the molasses (or treacle) over the butter.

4. Sift together the flour, baking soda, ginger, and salt.

5. Stir the dry mixture into the liquid mixture.

Here's a poem you can say while you are mixing:

"The spoon stirs up the birthday treat, cup by cup.

Let's put in the _____ ,

and stir it all up."

6. Roll the dough out, and place your stencil on top of it. Cut around it. Cut as many as you can.

7. Put the numbers on a cookie sheet and put raisins on them.

8. Bake for 8 to 10 minutes.

You can also serve your friends Birthday Lime Lick. Make this treat the day before the party also.

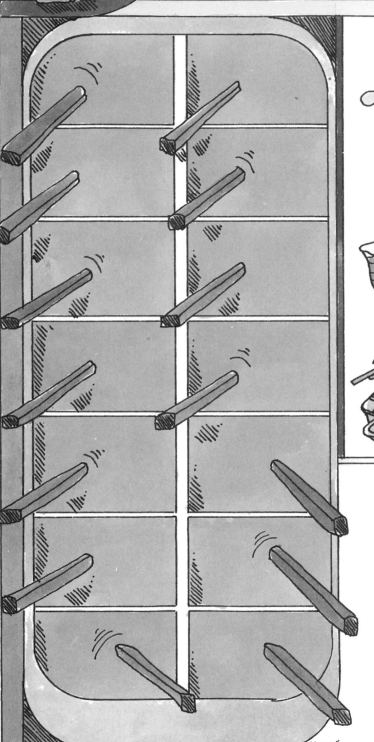

You need:

A saucepan

1 teaspoon gelatin

½ cup sugar

1½ cups of water

⅓ cup of lime juice

About 20 small sticks

2 ice cube trays

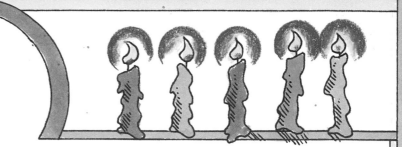

How to make enough for 8 friends:

1. Mix in a saucepan the gelatin, sugar, and water.

2. Boil for 3 minutes.

3. Add the lime juice.

4. Pour it into the ice cube trays. Put one stick in each of the cube sections.

5. Put the trays in the freezer.

When the party is over and your friends have gone home, here is something nice to do by yourself.
Some people believe you can tell what kind of person you are from the stars and planets. You have to find out where the stars and planets were when you were born. This is called astrology.

The year is broken up into twelve parts, called signs. They tell you where the stars and planets were on the day you were born.
You can find your sign. Look at the dates above each sign. Your birthday will fall between the two dates above one of the signs. That one is your sign.

March 21 to April 19
Aries, the Ram

April 20 to May 20
Taurus, the Bull

May 21 to June 21
Gemini, the Twins

June 22 to July 22
Cancer, the Crab

July 23 to August 22
Leo, the Lion

August 23 to September 22
Virgo, the Virgin

September 23 to October 23
Libra, the Scales

October 24 to November 21
Scorpio, the Scorpion

November 22 to December 21
Sagittarius, the Centaur

December 22 to January 19
Capricorn, the Goat

January 20 to February 18
Aquarius, the Water Carrier

February 19 to March 20
Pisces, the Fish

You love to play.
You have a lot of energy.

You are gentle and kind.
You like being at home.

You are like two people—
you change your mind a lot.
You like playing outside.

You are sensitive.
You love to love.

A lion is a leader.
You like being a leader, too.
You love adventure.

You ask a lot of questions.
You are a good thinker.

You like school work.
You are wise.

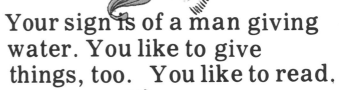

Your sign is of a man giving water. You like to give things, too. You like to read.

You trust people.
You like to write.

Your sign is scales because you balance what you want to do.
You are artistic.
You can be trusted.

You are strong.
You like puzzles.

You are unselfish.
You are a merry person.

After the party, you can make yourself some more presents. They can last a long time, maybe until your next birthday. You can make a Birthday Bank.

You need:

An empty salt container with a spout

A mixing bowl

A spoon

1 cup of white flour

1 cup of water

1 drop of food dye

A blunt knife

Birthday candles

Poster paints

A paintbrush

How to make it:

1. Peel the label off the salt container and open the spout.

2. Mix the flour and water in the mixing bowl.

3. Stir in one drop of food dye.

4. Spread the flour mixture on the salt container with the knife. Pretend you are frosting a cake.

5. Put the candles on top.

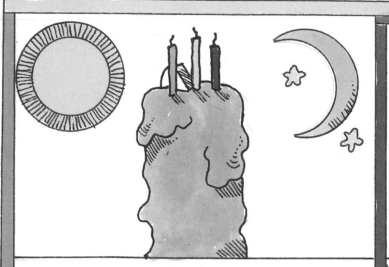
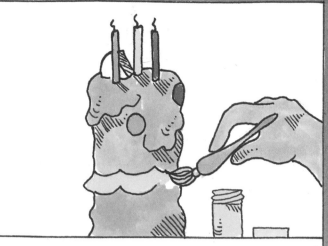

6. Let it dry for one day and one night.

7. Now you can paint it.

Open your Birthday Bank on your next birthday and you can buy yourself a present.

Would you like to make a Birthday Foot Chart?

<u>You need</u>:

A piece of construction paper big enough to stand on

Poster paint

A paintbrush

Crayons

Construction paper

Scissors

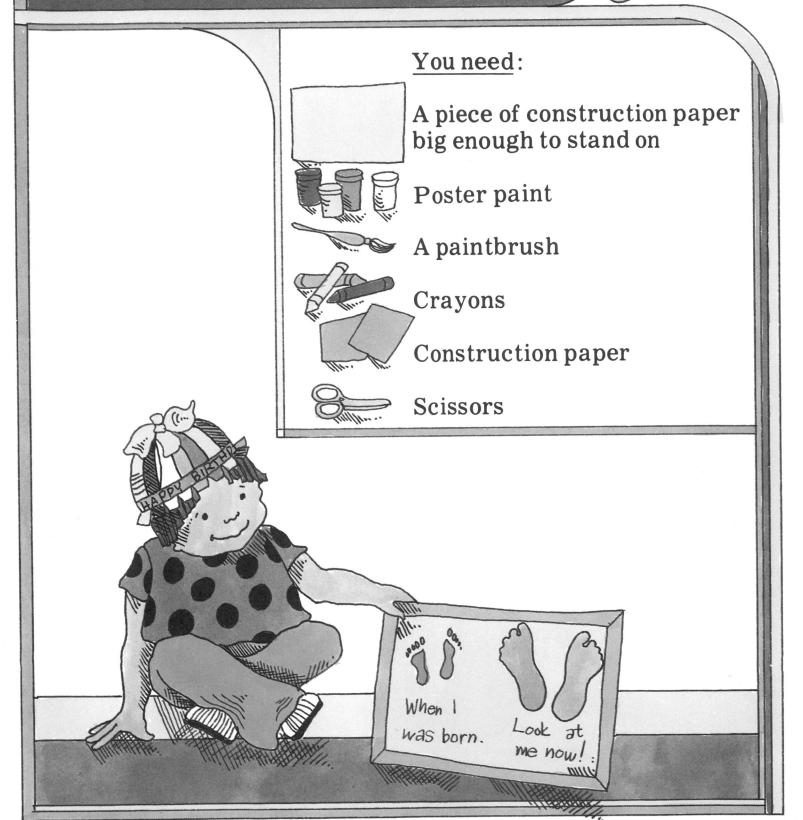

When I was born.

Look at me now!

41

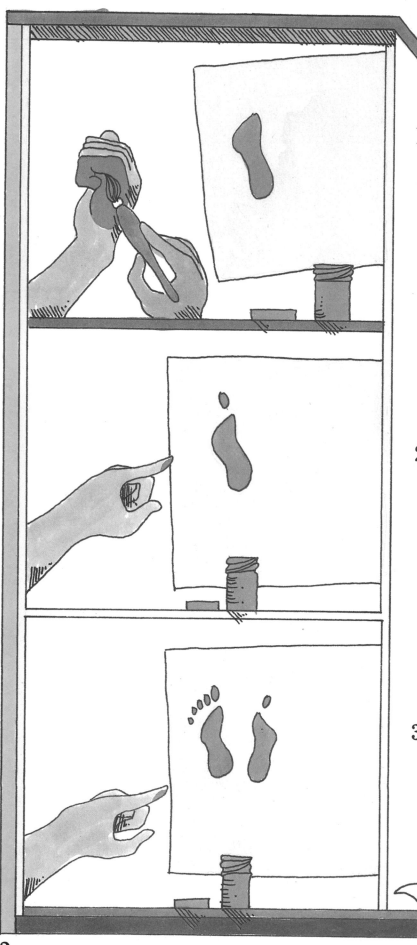

How to make it:

1. Poster paint the end of your fist like this. Press it down on the paper.

2. Put paint on the tip of your finger and make 5 toes.

3. Do the same thing with the other hand.

Don't they look like baby footprints?

42

4. Outline the shape of your foot while you stand on the paper, next to the baby footprints. Crayon them in.

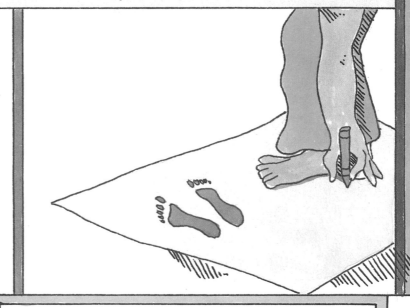

5. Write "When I was born" under the baby footprints. Write "Look at me now!" under your big footprints.

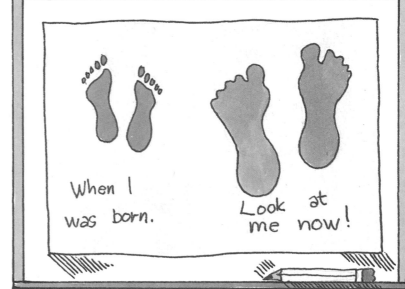

6. Make a frame out of the other construction paper. Now you can hang up your Birthday Foot Chart.

You can do this each year and watch your footprints get bigger and bigger.

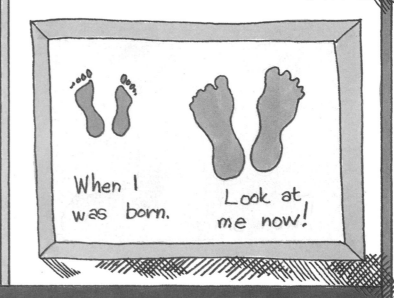

You can make a Birthday Panorama from the birthday cards you received.

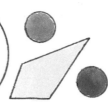

You need:

An old shoe box

Construction paper

Crayons

Glue

Scissors

Your birthday cards

How to make it:

1. Decorate the shoe box with the paper.

2. Cut out the pictures you like best on your cards, BUT CUT OUT A TAB on the bottom of the pictures, like this.

3. Put glue on the front of the tabs and bend them in, like this.

4. Arrange them in the box.

It would really be a lot of fun to plant an avocado tree on your birthday.

You need:

An avocado pit

3 toothpicks

A glass of water

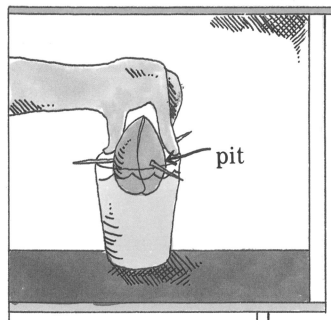

pit

How to do it:

1. Stick the toothpicks around the middle of the avocado pit.

2. Put it on the rim of the glass, **POINTED SIDE UP.**

3. Set it in a shady place. It will sprout in a few weeks.

4. When it has sprouted and has roots, you can plant it in a flower pot with dirt.

Your avocado tree will grow as you grow older.

And you will always remember when you planted it, on YOUR birthday.

Answer to page 20.

7